A Practical Guide to Getting It Right with Your Children

HOW TO BE A BETTER FATHER

STEPHEN MEDLOCK

TABLE OF CONTENTS

UNIT I

FATHERHOOD

Chapter

1

FUNDAMENTAL LAWS OF FATHERHOOD

Skeptical people said it couldn't be done. Fatherhood is too complicated, they cried, to be reduced to capsule form. But the complexity only added intrigue to my search for guiding principles.

After all the emotion, all the yelling, all the laughter, I have distilled the duties and demands down to a few.

Be Big

In spirit, that is.

Consider some of the guys who have gone before you: Father Times, The Founding Fathers, God the Father. It's a powerful tradition. The kids expect some stature from you. You can't give this role a walk-through. You've got to play it.

Now, this doesn't mean that you can choose any old vivid persona. After all, Genghis Khan was plenty vivid, and his kids didn't have an easy time.

But you can't be a blank slate. The kids ought to know what the old man would think about this or that. You are the anvil on which they hammer out their deal with the world. Be a presence in their lives—and their minds.

Be Small

Yes, this directly contradicts the first commandment. I told you, fatherhood is complicated.

Don't be so big that you suck all the air out of the room. Give your kids a little space to move around in, to test their thoughts and strengths. Take a back seat, figuratively speaking, three or four times a week. Say, "Maybe." Say, "I don't know."

Now and then, tell the kids you're sorry. There are plenty of things to apologize for: anger, inattention, bad career planning, lack of whatever. Mean it. Be sorry. You'll feel brand new.

Come Home

To be sure, the obligations of making a living can keep you out of the house. Lots of fathers have a day job and a night job. If that's your situation, God bless you, pal. You'll get no heat from me.

But if you can pay the bills without working double-shift, you've got to be home when you can.

You don't have to be playing catch all the time or even talking to the kids. But at least, be present. Get off the golf course. Head home. Nothing good can happen until you do.

Honor Thy Father and Mother

This is actually the biblical fifth commandment.

It's included here only because now that I'm one of the people getting the honoring, I like the sound of it much better than I did when I was a boy.

Bob and Weave

Stay light on your feet, Dad. Don't make too many hard and fast rules. Don't draw too many lines in the sand.

This doesn't mean anything goes; there are rules. It just means that fatherhood is an improvisation and that human hearts—both yours and the children's—have a way with compromise.

Don't insist on having your way with the kids just because the rest of the world isn't always overly interested in the sound of your voice. There is a difference between authority and power. Have the first; don't abuse the second.

Thou Shalt Not Dance

My own father once picked us up at a junior high school dance. As usual, he was wearing his wingtip shoes and that hat he got through the mail from Ireland.

As we were walking out of the gym, he actually did a few seconds of the hully-gully with a horrified Margie Costanzo. My sister still has nightmares about it.

If you've got to dance, dance with Mom in private. Don't embarrass everybody with your version of the Hustle.

Save Your Money, Big Man

You know all those corny proverbs about pennies saved? If you're not careful, the kids will send you to the poorhouse three dollars and twenty-nine cents at a time.

Think college tuition. Think down-payment on their starter homes.

Though it's true that money can't buy happiness, it can buy lots of other stuff. Believe in compound interest, tax-free growth. For God's sake, champ, be ready for emergencies.

Spend Your Money, Tightwad

You see what I'm after here, don't you? F. Scott Fitzgerald said the sign of a first-rate mind was the ability to have two opposite opinions at the same time. Never mind that he fell victim to drink. You're a first-rate mind, Dad.

Spring for the glowing monster trading cards. If you've got the money, pop for the musical princess crown.

What are you saving your money for, pal? College? Hah! You can't possibly save enough. There is the future, and then there is now. This is not a dress rehearsal. This is it.

Stay Off Amusement Park Rides

Even though you want to participate with the kids, to feel their gravity-defying thrill/terror/glee, you mustn't get on that ride with them.

I did in the summer of 1995, the Space Shuttle Whirl at Great Escape near Lake George, N.Y., and I've been a little queasy ever since. It's tough to be a good father when your nervous system is on the fritz.

Stay on the ground and wave

This is Their Life

I can’t say it any better than one of the most eminent psychiatrists of our time, Bruno Bettelheim: “We become upset when we believe we see in a child aspects of our own personalities of which we disapprove.”

Bang! On the money!

It’s tempting to make good on your own shortcomings through your children. Just because you didn’t make the varsity at North Salem High that doesn’t mean Stan Jr. has to. Help them follow their own path, not your road-not-taken.

Chapter

2

DIFFERENCE BETWEEN FATHER AND DAD

A father is the male parent of the child; its progenitor.

They share DNA with the child, but he may or may not share responsibility in the child's growth and development. Dad is a term of affection and familiarity. Dad is someone who actively participates in the child's growth and development.

There is a saying: "Any man can be a father, but it takes someone special to be a Daddy".

While in definition, both terms mean the same, their implications have changed over the years. A father is the male parent of the child; its progenitor. Traditional roles of a father dictate that fathers act in a protective, supportive and responsible way towards their children. Fathers who are active in the children's lives play a role in how the children grow up. They have an impact on the child's behavior, psychology and their development.

However, not all fathers are active in children's lives. There are many fathers who believe that once the child is born, their role is over. Of course, they are still the child's father, as they do share DNA with the child, but they do not share responsibility in the child's growth and development. He might pay the bills on time, he might supply the food and money, and he might provide for the family. However, if he does not even know his children, know their likes and dislikes, or what is going on with them, at school or personally, chances are the children will not consider him to be their dad.

Dad is a term of affection and familiarity. Dad is someone who actively participates in the child's growth and development. A dad fulfills all the responsibilities associated with the role, personal as well as societal and cultural. The dad may or may not be the biological father. He may be the adoptive father, the step-father, or just a nurturing male figure in the child's life, such as grandfathers and uncles, cousins and big brothers, family friends, who fulfill some of the father's responsibilities.

Research shows that an increased amount of father-child involvement may help increase a child's social stability, educational achievement, and their potential to have a solid marriage as an adult. The children may also be more curious about the world around them and develop greater problem-solving skills. So, even if fathers fulfill monetary responsibilities, they do not give the child these abilities. They do not fulfill their responsibilities to the child.

Dads are the one who is there for the child, when they need them, in good times and bad. They are the ones who will stay up with the child, the one who will attend the child's games and team practices. They are the ones who will take the children out for a holiday, teach them to ride a bike, drive a car and give them away at their marriage. They provide guidance, an open ear, and a caring heart.

The main difference between a father and a dad is that father is biological; however, a dad's relationship is emotional. Fathering is an act of nature, while, being a dad is all about nurture. It is much easier to become a father, many even do it unintentionally; however, it is much harder to commit to becoming a dad.

Still, these terms are subjective, depending on the usage in the family. A child may call the father a dad, despite not having a caring or nurturing relationship. Likewise, a child may call her father, 'father' at least in front of friends and family, despite him being the best father.

Personal experience with these terms may vary. Some may not even call their father, father or dad. They may have some other name or nickname, such as Da, Pa, Papa, Dada, etc. Some may even call their stepfathers by name, even though they may have a dad-child relationship.

Chapter

3

WHAT MAKES A BAD FATHER?

A bad father is a man who is not present in a child's life or who is in the child's life but is a bad influence. A bad father neglects his responsibilities to his family on many levels. He fails to provide a good masculine role model for his sons or a loving husband model for his daughters.

In the view of Flora Richards-Gustafson, a bad parent does not give his child or children unconditional love, independence, flexibility or a good example to follow.

Bad fathers can, by their influence, lead children to adopt some of the same negative traits and behaviors. If a father is abusive, violent, condescending or controlling, then he can damage his children's views of relationships and of the people around them.

A father who does not contribute to family life can be a burden rather than a necessary support. If he does not stand up for his family and protect them from harm, he is neglecting his primary duties. Bad fathers often create strained relationships with their children by providing too little affection and love, or by being otherwise absent from the children's lives. A closed-minded, strict parent who refuses to listen to his child is encouraging resentment of authority in that child. On the other hand, a father who is self-centered and a poor disciplinarian gives his child less respect for adults in general. Being a good father is not easy; it requires love, self-discipline and selflessness. Good fathers do not give in to their bad impulses and try to do the best they can for their families.

10 Qualities of A Good Dad

Men are playing a more active role in parenting. They don't just take the role of provider, protector, and disciplinarian in the family.

Today the role of fatherhood has evolved and along with it men are now embracing a whole load of new skills and values.

How do men influence their kid's development?

By looking at how our kids see us we learn something about ourselves! Primary school kids in the US were asked to describe what makes a good dad. They came up with the following:

- "A good dad makes you feel safe"
- "A good dad can protect his children from getting hurt"
- "A good dad knows how to keep the bad guys away"
- "A good dad always listens to Mum"

I'm not sure about the last comment! However, protection and safety emerge as important for our kids. The research further explored the way children tend to see their dads as follows:

- Safe
- Strong

- Comforting
- Protecting
- The hero
- Teacher
- Wise and knowledgeable

The notion that 'just being there' may not be enough to influence our kids' growth and development. Researchers have developed and defined quite specific characteristics or attitudes of fatherhood in relation to the developmental needs of children.

Here are 10 qualities that are proving significant, in helping our kids grow to be resilient, healthy individuals. In no particular order:

1. Dependability

Being there through thick and thin. This is not just being present and correct. It's about being consistently available for our kids through good times and bad.

2. Involvement

Being personally engaged in our kids' lives, interests, hopes and dreams on a daily basis. Being curious and attentive requires us to put our distractions to one side.

3. Compassion

Showing compassion, hope and belief when our child needs it most. Compassion is a state of mind or attitude that really helps us to feel connected and close to the human experience of being a child.

4. Valuing of mother

Showing respect and love of our kids' mother. This isn't about just always agreeing with mum! Valuing is similar to validating our partner for who they are with all their imperfections. Showing love and respect requires action, not just thoughts, and teaches our sons and daughters how to be treated.

5. Empathy

Listening empathically in order to be understanding, present and engaged. Putting ourselves into the shoes of others enables them to feel heard, respected and valued. Even if we don't completely get it, or even like it!

6. Being verbally expressive

To clearly communicate, uphold guidelines, being tough yet fair, without belittling or being controlling.

7. Being human

To own mistakes, be open to feedback, and teach that growth is a lifelong endeavour. So, dad (and mum) get it wrong, sometimes! I reckon teaching our kids to be human means we have to show our own humanity, as often as possible.

8. Honesty

Teach and live by the values of honesty and integrity.

9. Playfulness

Showing delight in our children through fun and play. The benefits of dads playing has been researched, particularly the rough and tumble play. It teaches our kids to regulate their feelings and accept limits and boundaries.

10. Being industrious

Model a healthy work ethic as a source of personal accomplishment and satisfaction. This isn’t necessarily associated only with work; it’s a valuable attitude toward tasks in general.

Traits of A Great Father

A good father makes all the difference in a child's life. He's a pillar of strength, support, and joy. His work is endless and, sometimes, thankless. But in the end, it shows in the sound, well-adjusted children he raises.

A good father loves his children, but he doesn't let them get away with everything. He might disapprove of his children's misdeeds, using tough love to prove a point, but he does so through the power of his words.

A good father realizes that his children are human, and that making mistakes is part of growing up. Spending money recklessly, getting into minor car accidents, getting drunk for the first time, even dating questionable people are rites of passage, and a good father recognizes this. However, he makes it clear that repeated irresponsibility won't be tolerated.

1. He Teaches His Children to Appreciate Things

A good father never lets his children take what they have for granted. From the food on the table to the good education he's paying for, a good father will make his children see the value in everything they have. He will ask his child to get a job to help pay for a part of his first car, and take the time to illustrate how important a good education is. He doesn't let his kids treat him like an ATM. Instead, he teaches his kids to appreciate important purchases.

2. He's Open-Minded

A good father understands that times, people, and tastes change over the years, and doesn't try to maintain some gold standard of his own time. For instance, he realizes that body piercings are more commonplace than before and that people talk more candidly about personal issues. In other words, he allows his children to be citizens of their day and age.

3. He Accepts That His Kids Aren't Exactly Like Him

Everyone is different and a father knows this well. He won't expect his kids to live the same kind of life he does, and do the same kind of work. He also respects their values and opinions, as long as they don't harm the family or anyone else.

4. He Spends Quality Time With His Children

A dad knows how to have fun with his kids, too, taking them out to games, movies, and supporting their sports, hobbies, or activities by showing up and taking an interest. He takes the time to listen to his kids and have a good, easy chat with them. He also makes time to help them with their homework, every night if necessary.

5. He Leads by Example

A good father is above the old "do as I say, not as I do" credo. He will not smoke if he doesn't want his kids to, and definitely won't drink heavily. He teaches them to deal with conflict with a family member and with others by being firm but reasonable at the same time.

A good father also illustrates the importance of affection by professing his love for their mother in front of them. And he won't fight with her in their presence. In all, he adheres to the values he'd like his children to follow.

6. He's Supportive and Loyal

Although he may be a football fanatic, if his child doesn't share his love for the game, he accepts it. He may be loyal to his alma mater and dream of having his kid follow his legacy, but if his son prefers to study abroad, he'll support his decision to take a different path.

A good father is also his children's public defender, standing up for them when needed. He waits for privacy to administer discipline. A safety net, a good father is also the person his kids turn to when things go wrong.

7. He Challenges His Kids

A father wants his children to be the best they can be, and gives them challenges that help them grow as human beings. This means giving them some liberty to face setbacks and resolve conflicts on their own. Or it could be a task, such as building something for the house.

If a father wants his children to take over the family business, he teaches them how to keep it flourishing — provided that's the path they want to take.

8. He Teaches His Kids Lessons

From teaching how to shave to encouraging them to be thoughtful and considerate, a father molds his kids into well-rounded members of society. He especially instructs them in proper etiquette, on being honest, and on being thankful.

9. He Protects His Family, No Matter What

A father will do whatever he can for his family. He'll take a second job to help support the family when necessary, and he'll do what he can to keep his family out of harm's way.

10. He Shows Unconditional Love

This is the greatest quality of a good father. Even though he gets upset at his children's faults and may lament that they did not attain what he hoped for them, a father loves his children no less for it.

There are few things as valuable as a father who will do everything he can, and provide all the tools he has so that his children can become better than him.

Chapter

4

WORDS TO DESCRIBE A GOOD FATHER

1. appreciated
2. balding
3. best
4. blessed
5. brave
6. brilliant
7. busy
8. careful
9. caring
10. clever
11. coaching
12. compassionate
13. confident
14. considerate
15. cool
16. courageous
17. dependable
18. devoted
19. doting
20. encouraging
21. knowledgeable
22. loved
23. loving
24. loyal

25.lucky
26.motivating
27.one-of-a-kind
28.parental
29.patient
30.positive
31.practical
32.protecting
33.protective
34.proud
35.reliable
36.respected
37.responsible
38.sacrificing
39.selfless
40.sentimental
41.fraternal
42.fun
43.funny
44.generous
45.gentle
46.giving
47.grateful
48.great
49.guiding
50.handsome
51.handy
52.hardworking
53.helpful
54.hilarious
55.honest
56.indebted
57.inspirational
58.inspiring
59.intelligent
60.kind
61.smart
62.soft-hearted
63.special
64.stable
65.stern
66.strong

67.strong-willed
68.super
69.supportive
70.sweet
71.teaching
72.tenderhearted
73.thoughtful
74.trusting
75.unafraid
76.understanding
77.watchful
78.wise
79.wonderful

UNIT II

FATHERHOOD AND TOXICITY

Chapter 5

SIGNS OF A TOXIC FATHER

By the time you reach adulthood, you probably have some serious thoughts about your upbringing. Most parents legitimately try their best, but there are unfortunately some exceptions to this rule. Knowing the signs you have a toxic father can help you heal from past trauma, as well as refrain from repeating these mistakes with your own kids.

First, though, it's important to understand what makes a relationship toxic in the first place. "In the context of parenting, the word toxic means they are hindering their child's development and causing harm.

Often these parents experienced neglect or dysfunction while growing up, then go on to replicate these maladaptive behaviors when raising their own children. Toxic relationships are marked by disrespect and devaluation. It's hard to feel good about yourself when around this person.

Fortunately, you aren't doomed to repeat your father's behaviors. Simply knowing the signs of toxic behavior, and being aware of your own actions, can go a long way.

Plus, you don't have to give the toxic person a place in your current life. Establishing and maintaining distance may be the healthiest choice in a toxic relationship that is not likely to change. Distance can be physical (you do not see them) or mental (certain topics are off limits or mental boundaries are drawn to protect oneself).

You can also explore the option of counseling to address these pain points and find a healthier way to parent your own children. Growing up with a toxic parent is rough on any child, but you can identify the signs and move on to a happier future.

He's Disrespectful

Does it feel like you'll never measure up to your father's demands? When someone consistently and intentionally makes you feel less than, not worthy, and disrespects you and your life, it is a toxic relationship. There's a difference between expressing a genuine concern for your well-being or simply bashing every choice you make.

He Gives You The Silent Treatment

There are plenty of healthy ways to address conflict, and the silent treatment is not one of them. In general, the silent treatment is a sign of abusive control or punishment, as explained in Psych Central. It's a frustrating and ineffective tactic.

He Screams Threats

Out-of-control threats are not only the sign of a toxic father, but they are also wildly ineffective. In fact, constant threats may cause older kids to pursue disruptive behaviors. Verbal hostility is real, and potentially damaging.

He Has Substance Misuse Issues

Does your father seem to turn into a different (meaner) person after drinking? As it turns out, alcohol abuse is another potential sign of a toxic parent.

Issues around substance misuse can certainly affect a person's ability to parent.

He Doesn't Want You To Grow Up

Taking the regular steps toward adulthood should be celebrated. But in some cases, the parent tries to keep the child dependent on them even when the child is an adult or becoming an adult. In reality, growing up and maturing is simply natural.

He Has Violent Outbursts

Sure, anger can get the best of everyone now and then. But a toxic person may regularly experience violent outbursts and then blame you for the reaction. This kind of a bad temper is totally destructive.

He Provides Conditional Love

Ideally, a parent's love is unconditional. But in a more toxic scenario, the parent only shows approval or love when the child conforms to who the parent wants them to be. There's no space to just be yourself.

He Inspires Fear

Did you have to walk on eggshells growing up? If your father used fear as a manipulation tactic, then this is almost certainly a sign of toxic parenting. Remember, fear does not equal love or respect.

He's Narcissistic

As far as narcissists are concerned, they're the center of the world. So of course, parents with narcissistic tendencies can be toxic as well. Even after reaching adulthood, you may feel like your father's needs are larger than life — and far more important than your own.

He's Aloof

Speaking of unchecked narcissistic traits, narcissistic fathers who are aloof and removed from their children probably did not provide the warmth and care needed by kids, according to Psychology Today. It's potentially damaging.

He's Controlling

Did your dad monitor and manipulate your every move? Overly controlling parents may lead to kids with higher levels of depression and dissatisfaction. If this sounds all too familiar, then you may want to seek counseling for support.

Other Signs You Have A Toxic Father

He compares you to your siblings

You and your older sister are two completely different people. But because she’s a doctor with three kids and you’re a single teacher, your dad loves to try to pit the two of you against each other. Your sister takes the high road, but your dad’s constant teasing still makes you feel insecure and attacked.

He doesn't respect boundaries

You love your dad, but he's always had a hard time knowing his place. He's made a habit of showing up at your house, unannounced, expecting to be able to stay for dinner. Because you love him, you give in, but even after asking him to stop popping in without calling, he continues to do it.

He insists on being right

Your dad has hated every person you've ever dated, and it's starting to feel like no one is going to be good enough. He has similar opinions about your career goals, friends and pretty much everything else. If you've articulated that you're happy with your life and the people in it and he still won't stay out of your business, then your relationship with your dad could be verging on (if not already) toxic.

You feel exhausted after spending time or speaking with him

Do you feel totally spent every time you interact with your dad? We're not talking about feeling like you need to be by yourself for a little while—something that can happen even with people we love being around. Interacting with a toxic person can leave you feeling defeated since their dramatic, needy and high-maintenance tendencies can suck the energy right out of you.

He consistently plays the victim

Sometimes, parents can't help but guilt trip their kids. ("What do you mean, you aren't coming home for Thanksgiving?") But there's a difference between expressing disappointment and creating a toxic environment by blaming everyone else for their feelings. If your dad refuses to talk to you for a week because you've decided to spend next Thanksgiving with friends, you could be in toxic territory.

He tries to compete with you

Every time you call your dad to talk about a promotion at work or a potty-training breakthrough with your kid, he inevitably steers the conversation to be about his illustrious career or his methods of raising you. Any healthy relationship should be a two-way street, and if your dad is incapable of celebrating your wins—big or small—it's a sign that there's an issue.

Everything is about him

You just got off a 45-minute phone call with your dad only to realize that he didn't ask you a single question about your life or how you're doing. If he was dealing with an important issue or had some exciting news, that's one thing. But if this happens pretty much every time you talk, then this relationship could be toxic.

There are always strings attached

Sure, dad will pick up the grandkids from school, but you'll never hear the end of how lucky you are to have his help…followed by an immediate request to reorganize his basement. We're not suggesting our parents should do every little thing for us, but you should be able to ask for a favor without having him hold it over your head or immediately ask for something unreasonable in return.

He’s impossible to please

You’re constantly bending over backward to please everyone in your life—your dad included. Most people are thankful for your flexibility and help, but your dad seems to always want more. If you consistently feel like you’re coming up short in his eyes, it’s not an issue with how you’re doing things, it’s on him.

Chapter

6

REASONS WHY SOME FATHERS AND SONS DO NOT GET ALONG?

The relationship between a male and his father is one of the building blocks for the son's emotional stability later in life. According to a study by California State University-Fullerton, men that had positive childhood relationships with their fathers are more able to handle stress and emotional distress later in life than those that didn't.

Unfortunately, not every male enjoys a nurturing, positive relationship with his father. There are a variety of reasons why some fathers and sons don't get along.

The Apple and the Tree

The popular saying, "The apple doesn't fall far from the tree," isn't always true. And even when it is, that doesn't always mean dad and son will always see eye to eye.

Some sons are simply the polar opposites of their fathers, resulting sometimes in feelings of disappointment on the father's side and rejection on the son's end.

And in those cases where the son is a reincarnation of his father personality-wise, that doesn't guarantee a jovial relationship. This relates largely to the longstanding theory that the flaws you're most annoyed by in others are the ones you also possess.

Divorce

Divorce is another factor that can strain, and even destroy, the relationship between a father and son. According to "The Custody Evaluation Handbook" by Barry Bricklin, Ph.D., males whose parents divorced are three times more likely than their female counterparts to grow up maladjusted and aggressive-insecure. This, naturally, can lead to strained relationships between fathers and sons, especially when the son feels the father is somehow at fault for the deterioration of the family unit.

Immaturity

While many boys idolize their fathers, that can change once the teenage years arrive. That's the stage during which a young male is attempting to form his own identity. Rebellion again authority—often one's parents—is common, and clash often ensues. This, however, often changes as the son matures and comes to realize that he didn't, in fact, know everything, and begins to realize his father was right about a lot more than he'd realized as an adolescent.

Absent Fathers

If you grew up without your father living with you or playing a significant role in your life, you know the reconciliation can be difficult. Though many absentee fathers attempt to reunite with their sons later in life, there's often awkwardness between the two and the sons often hold a grudge. According to the U.S. Census Bureau, children in fatherless homes are five times more likely to be poor than are other children. And the U.S. Department of Health and Human Services reports that children with absentee fathers are far more likely to abuse substances.

Mending the Rift

Even with the problems that exist between fathers and sons, there are always opportunities to improve these relationships.

By sharing in activities or even simply spending time together, fathers and sons can learn to overcome their differences. It may take time, but father-son relationships do not always have to be on bad terms.

Chapter

7

HOW TO STRENGTHEN A FATHER SON RELATIONSHIP

In life, we tend to invest time and money into the things we care about and when it comes to father-son relationships this principle is especially relevant. But the father-son relationship can be complex. Fathers and sons with widely different interests can find it hard to relate to one another. Sometimes, dads and sons feel competitive against one another.

Other times, communication issues are compounded when both want a better father-son relationship but neither one knows quite how to go about it. If you find yourself in this situation, here are some key elements to creating and building a strong father-son relationship.

Set a Good Example

There are many things you can do to develop a strong bond with your son. Whether we realize it or not, sons learn about being a man primarily by watching their fathers. A father's influence on their son's personal development is often unseen but nonetheless real.

As young men watch their fathers interact with others including their partner, they learn about respect (or disrespect), about how men interact with others, and about how men should deal with conflict and differences. Understanding that a father's influence on their son is unmatched will help you think more deeply about your relationship with your son and take your responsibility as a good role model seriously.

Spend Time Together

As a father, make sure that you allow for some one-on-one time with your son. This time together lets your son know that they're important to you, especially if you make time for them amidst a very busy schedule.

Carving out time together also communicates that they are a priority in your life and that you enjoy being with them.

While they are young, you can engage in boisterous play outside, read books, build with legos, or play a game. Once they are older and have more defined interests, try to participate in the things they enjoy, too.

Whether your son loves basketball or debate, find ways to get involved. Play hoops in the driveway or learn how to be a debate judge when they're in high school. Some of your best memories will be of those times you spent together doing something they're passionate about. Plus, evidence suggests that a father's involvement in activities supports their son's cognitive, linguistic, and socio-emotional development.1 Here are some things fathers and sons can do together.

- **Work on a hobby together.** Some fathers enjoy time with their sons when they find a hobby they can do together. Whether that involves collecting memorabilia, building model airplanes, gardening, or restoring an old car, find something you are both excited about and do it together.

- **Participate in father-son activities.** Local communities and schools often organize father-son events like fishing derbies, game nights, and more, so be sure to take advantage of these events. The Boy Scouts also provide an opportunity to bond. Father-son duos can camp, hike, work on merit badges, and spend quality time together. You could even consider getting involved as an adult Scouter volunteer.
- **Volunteer for your son's after school activities.** If your son is involved in extracurricular activities, look for opportunities to get involved. For instance, you can volunteer to be a timer at a swim meet, a line judge at a volleyball game, a chaperone for a band competition, or an usher at the school play. Regardless of your son's activities and interests, there are always ways to get involved.

- **Play a sport together.** Although the mention of sports conjures up images of traditional sports like football, basketball, and baseball, don't let that limit you. There are many sports that fathers and sons can do together like running, hiking, rock climbing, skateboarding, volleyball, swimming, and even ice hockey.

Develop Shared Interests

Father-son relationships can feel strained at times, especially if your interests appear to be polar opposites. With a little effort, though, you can usually find something that you both find interesting. These shared interests allow you to discover some commonality while maximizing the time you spend together doing something you both enjoy.

Finding common interests benefits your father-son relationship in a number of ways. For instance, sharing an interest with someone allows you insight into who the person is.

Common interests also become a vehicle for bonding by giving you something to talk about and do together that you both enjoy.

If your son is younger, try different things together until you land on something you both enjoy doing. And if your son is older, talk to them about their interests to see if it sparks something in you as well. Here are some common things that fathers and sons might share an interest in, but don't limit yourself to this list.

- **Music:** Some fathers and sons both have a passion for music. Whether that means attending concerts together, following particular bands, building playlists, or even creating your own band, there are a number of ways you can bond over your shared interest in music.
- **Sports:** Following a favorite sports team is a classic father-son activity. Aside from watching the games on TV or attending a game in person, fathers and sons have been bonding over baseball, basketball, football, hockey, and more for years. If sports are something you and your son share a

passion for, look for ways to build on this shared interest.

- **Outdoor activities:** When it comes to the great outdoors, the options are endless. Perhaps you both enjoy hiking, fishing, and camping, or maybe you both enjoy gardening, bird watching, or stargazing, the key is to explore different things until you find something you both enjoy.
- **Cooking:** Some fathers and sons find that they both enjoy cooking, grilling, or even baking. If this is a shared interest for you and your son, you can spend a few days a month experimenting with flavors and creating new recipes. You can even enter cooking competitions together. Doing so, will build memories to last a lifetime.
- **Games:** Whether you play board games or video games, if you and your son both enjoy games you have countless options for father son bonding time. Nothing builds a relationship more than playing a game together. Aside from the fun you get from a little friendly competition, playing a game together

is the perfect vehicle for having meaningful conversations. And it's these conversations that allow you to build a deeper relationship with your son.

Work Together on a Project

There is something magical for a boy about being involved in something bigger than themself. Plus, these big, visible projects can really help strengthen a father and son bond.

Some dads and sons build planter boxes, landscape a backyard, build a vacation cabin, participate in Habitat for Humanity, or head off on a big summer biking vacation. Whatever it is, a bigger-than-life project done together can create a bond that will last a long time and make memories you will talk about together for decades.

To come up with a project you and your son can do together, think about what you both enjoy or community issues you are passionate about when developing a project. If you're having trouble coming up with ideas, here are a few tips to get your creative juices flowing.

- **Look for service opportunities.** Whether you work on an Eagle Scout project together or you choose a charitable foundation to support, completing a service project together is a great way to bond with your son while learning the importance of giving back.
- **Plan an adventure.** Some fathers and sons enjoy going on an adventure together like biking across the country or walking the Appalachian Trail. You also can make it a goal to visit all the baseball parks in the country or try white water rafting in a variety of locations.
- **Remodel or build something.** Sometimes the best way to bond with your son is to build something together. What's more, your project can be as big or as small as you want it to be. For instance, you can build a bird feeder, flower boxes, an elevated garden, or display shelves for your memorabilia. Or, if you're really ambitious, you could always remodel a room in your home creating a cool space that the two of you can enjoy together later.

Listen

Starting from an early age, it's important that fathers learn how to listen to their sons without judgment and without trying to fix things too soon. Doing so, will go a long way to building a lasting relationship and developing an effective communication style.

To encourage your son to open up, look for opportunities to be with your son when you can just listen to what's on their mind or what they have to say. Fishing together, going to a sporting event, or taking a road trip can all be effective ways to create a listening environment.

Commit to spending 75% to 80% of the time engaged in active listening. Here are some tips on how you can effectively engage in active listening.

- **Give your son your full attention.** Whether your son comes to you with a question or they're talking while you're out on the lake, it's important that you give your son your full attention. Make eye contact and pay attention to their words without interrupting or offering advice.

- **Stop what you're doing.** When your child is talking, it's important that you stop what you're doing and pay attention. This may mean putting your phone down or turning away from the computer. Of course, if you're driving or doing something you cannot stop at the moment, do your best to communicate that they have your full attention like turning off the radio in the car.
- **Reflect back what they're saying.** A hallmark of active listening is the ability to repeat back what the other person is saying. Ensure your son knows that you understand what they're saying as well as how the situation makes them feel. If you are unsure, it's OK to ask questions for clarification but watch how you phrase the question as well as your tone of voice. You don't want your questions to come off like you're irritated, interrogating them, or being judgmental.

Have Conversations

Our children are bombarded with negative messages all around them. Just watching commercials on television can create a sense of inadequacy in our sons. They probably are not quite as strong, may not have six pack abs, or be quite as good looking as the guys they see on television.

As they grow up, they are forced to navigate and wrestle with a lot of big issues. For this reason, fathers need to have regular conversations about those big issues. Here's a brief overview of some of the topics you need to make sure you are talking about.

- **Sex:** Take the time to talk to your son about sex and relationships. Being open to having these conversations will help your son develop better attitudes about sex and romantic partners in general. Be sure to also have age-appropriate conversations about everything from sexting to consent.
- **Relationships:** Talk to your son about healthy friendships and relationships. Make sure they know what constitutes healthy dating as well as what would be considered toxic or abusive behavior.

- **Money:** Teaching your son how to handle money is one of the most important skills you can provide them with. Discuss the importance of saving, budgeting, and investing while giving them opportunities to practice their skills.
- **Social media:** When it comes to social media, it's important to teach your son the basics of digital etiquette before they even get a social media account. As they get older, be sure they know what constitutes cyberbullying as well as how important it is to manage their image online. Additionally, it's never too early to help them do a social media audit and clean up their accounts from time to time.
- **Peer pressure:** Talk to your son about the risks of peer pressure and what they can do if they're pressured to do something they're not comfortable with, especially when it comes to juuling, drinking alcohol, and using drugs. Equip them with the tools needed to respond to peer pressure in a healthy way.

- **Spirituality:** Helping a son be grounded spiritually is an important role for a father. Whatever your faith tradition, help your son understand the deeper meaning of life. If you don't have a faith tradition, help them look at things deeper than on the surface.

Focusing on your son, spending positive time together, and talking about life lessons, scattered with a large dose of quiet and engaged listening, will help you develop a nurturing and meaningful relationship with your son. Your efforts also will help your son form attitudes that allow them to develop into an upstanding person in the richest sense of the word.

Chapter 8

FATHER-DAUGHTER BONDING ACTIVITIES

Several years ago, I took my five-year-old daughter to a Father-Daughter Dance. When we left the dance towards the end of the night I asked her if she would like to take a walk along the river. So we walked hand in hand and eventually the path ended. There was no one around so I took out my iPhone and started playing a song. Then I put the iPhone in my dress shirt pocket and asked her to dance. Since that night we have passed the place where we danced many times. Every time she points it out, "Look Daddy! That's where we danced!"

That small, but significant, activity bonded us together. We have talked about it often. The big things are great, but many times it's the little father-daughter activities that help form a bond. With that in mind, here are 7 father-daughter bonding activities.

1. Special Handshake

Make up a special handshake that you only do with each other. Work on it together and get it just right. If you do, it could be something you do for a lifetime. She'll never forget it and it will make her feel special.

2. Overnight Trip

Take her away, just the two of you. It doesn't have to be expensive. However, make it somewhere you know she would enjoy. You could take her camping if she is into that. Have some bucket list activities to do during the day. Then at night when you lay down for bed break out some questions to talk about. Have a good mixture of fun ones and serious life ones. This also may be a good time to discuss sex, dating, and marriage. I've heard of fathers using opportunities like this to give their daughters a purity ring to remind them to wait until marriage before sex. It's up to you what you do with the time. Either way, getting away together will be a bonding experience.

3. Playing Games

Play games together. Nothing creates a bond like looking into each other's eyes which is why I like to have staring contests with my daughter. Play 20 questions and see what she comes up with. Whatever she chooses for you to guess will communicate what is important to her. Try charades. It will help with your non-verbal communication. When you are in the car together, play iSpy. Games are fun and an easy way to interact.

4. Dancing

Take your daughter to a father-daughter dance. Get dressed up and take pictures. Then make sure you take her out on the dance floor a couple of times. Learn to dance so you can lead her. You want to make her feel secure. There are plenty of Youtube videos that can show you some simple steps if you rhythmically challenged. If there aren't any dances coming up, then simply turn on some music in your living room. Or you can take her for a walk like I did and play a song on your phone. It's a memory she'll talk about for a long time.

5. A Restaurant that is an Event

Take her out for a special dinner. However, make sure the meal is an event. Japanese steakhouses put on a great show, fire, spatula flipping, and great food. Perhaps take her to a dinner theater, as long as the show is appropriate for her age, or take her to a drive-in movie (with dinner). Just make sure it is something out of the ordinary. Make sure it is something she will remember.

6. Her Favorite Activity

Do her favorite activity, whatever that may be. Observe her or, better yet, ask her if she could one thing with you what would it be. Then do that thing. At least for that hour or even a couple of hours, make it your favorite thing. For example, my daughter's favorite subject is Winnie the Pooh, especially Tigger. We could have a Winnie the Pooh Day where we have a picnic with her stuffed animals (plenty of honey), read some of the books, and end the day with a Winnie the Pooh movie marathon. What is your daughter's favorite thing? What themes and activities could you plan for a couple of hours or even a day?

7. Have a "Yes" Night

"It's important that we communicate to our daughters that they are worthy of attention and investment."

You need to be brave for this one. In the movie Yes Man with Jim Carrey, he basically has to say yes to everything. Tell your daughter that you are going to have a "Yes" night. Whatever activity she asks to do your answer has to be "yes." There need to be two rules associated with this night, however. One, nothing unsafe or against the law. Two, it needs to be considerate of others and not involve purchases that will hurt the family budget. Otherwise, go for it! I guarantee she will be talking about this night forever.

Whether you do some or all of these activities, you'll not only bond with your daughter, you'll set an expectation of how men should treat her. It's important that we communicate to our daughters that they are worthy of attention and investment.

UNIT III

GETTING BETTER AS A FATHER

Chapter

9

HOW TO BE A GOOD HUSBAND FOR A HAPPY MARRIAGE

As the excitement of wedding and honeymoon fades away, and you adjust to the wind and grind of real life, you realise that you have a partner to share in your joys and sorrows. Slowly, you become so used to each other that romance your romance starts dwindling. The vows that are made during the wedding ceremonies are not always followed through by people, but if you are the type of man who wants to really be the perfect husband to the woman you cherish, it is not too late to rekindle the spark and make your woman feel that you love her.

Tips to Become a Good Husband

Being a good husband is not something that comes naturally to most men. It often means putting yourself second and your wife first, which is something a lot of people take a little getting used to. Here are some tips to help you become a good husband to your wife.

1. Be Her Best Friend

A married couple is much more than just man and wife; they are best friends. You are partners in life, so it is best to get into the habit of going to the other first when something important happens in your life. Just the way you would pick up your phone to tell your friend all about the exciting event that happened, your first instinct should be to tell your wife because she is your closest and dearest friend. In the same way, if she comes to you with something, you should be able to share in her feelings about it and help her if she needs it.

2. Be Protective

To show your wife that you love her, be there for her. Be protective but never abuse her. Some men ignore if someone else insults their wife, but we know you are not the same. You love your wife and it's time you show her that. If someone insults your wife, protect her. You need to show that you support your wife and don't tolerate others disrespecting her. Never tolerate if someone insults or says mean jokes at your wife. Let people know that you are always at your wife's side, come what may.

3. Look After Yourself Physically

Most men don't care about their physical appearance once they are married. They stop putting any kind of effort into their appearance after they become too comfortable with each other. This can sometimes be what kills romance in a marriage. Make an effort to look good for your wife. She will appreciate it because she knows you are going through the effort for her.

4. Respect Her Beliefs

If you are both from the same religious background, it will be easy to share in her religious faith, but if you are from different backgrounds, there can always be respect for what she believes in. You should never make your wife feel silly for what she believes in, even if you don't believe in the same. Let your wife know that you respect her beliefs.

5. Show Love to Her

Men aren't the most sensitive bunch, and while it can be challenging for some to open up and show their love, it is a worthwhile endeavour. Most women love romance and like it when their husbands shower their love on them, so remember to be romantic with your wife once in a while. Show your love to her by giving her random kisses throughout the day or hugging her and telling her that you love her. These little acts will brighten her day.

6. Support Her

If your wife has a goal she wants to work towards, do everything that you can to support her. Don't laugh at her dreams because that will only break her spirit. You are the one person in the world who she should feel she can get support from, even if the rest of the world thinks she is silly. So, stand up for her. Make her believe that she can do anything she wants to do. She will love you even more.

7. Accept Her Faults

Men and women all have their flaws and faults, but true love is accepting the bad with the good. Focus on all the good things about her and ignore the things you don't like. If it is something that really bothers you, talk to her about it, or just learn to accept it. There may be things about you that she needs to learn to accept as well.

8. Don't Lose The Romance

If you have been married for a while, it is easy for the romance to die out as time moves on. As her husband, do your part when it comes to holding on to the romance. Don't let it die. Take her out for a date or surprise her with flowers and a romantic night at a hotel, the choices are endless.

9. Talk Things Through

Every couple has disagreements, but the ones who learn to talk things through instead of becoming angry or bitter about it are the ones whose relationship lasts long. Learning to respect each other's opinions is very important in a marriage, and learning to communicate without screaming and shouting at each other will save your marriage and give your children a more secure home life.

10. Take Care of Your Wife

If your wife falls sick or needs you to look after something, make sure you do it with your best efforts. Looking after each other through sickness and health is a part of your marriage vows and not something to be taken lightly. A good wife would do anything to look after her husband in her way, and in the same way, a good husband does his best to look after his wife's needs.

Qualities and Characteristics of a Good Husband

Here are some characteristics and qualities that every good husband has:

1. Passionate

A good husband is not just passionate when it comes to the physical aspect of marriage, but he is also passionate about small things. Women really appreciate men who take the efforts to like things that she does or who support them in their hobbies and passions. This is the basic quality of a good husband.

2. Trustworthy

A man who loves his wife makes sure that she trusts him. He never gives his wife a chance to doubt him or feel insecure. If you love your wife, be sure never to give her any reason not to trust you. Let her know that she can trust you with anything.

3. He is there for His Kids

A good husband loves his kids. Although it might be difficult for you to play with your kids after coming from work, but if you love your kids you will do it. By having fun with children you make your wife believe that you are in this together. And she will take pride in you that you because you are a good father.

4. Compassionate

A man who can feel for others is very appealing to women, so be a compassionate man and show you care. It can be towards your wife and others as well. The more compassion you show, the more of a hero you will look like to her.

5. Compromising

Marriage is hard work and sometimes the two of will not want to agree on a specific course of action. But a man who wants to make his relationship work is ready to compromise. There will be times when your wife may sacrifice her own position to make you happy, so you should learn to be able to compromise and come up with solutions that the both of you can agree on.

6. Loyal

A good husband is loyal to his wife. He never lets her feel that she is not good enough for him. If you love your wife, be loyal to her. Don't ever make her feel that you are not true to her, else it will break her heart.

7. Honest

An honest man makes for a wonderful husband. Telling your wife the truth, not hiding things from her and involving her in every aspect of your life will earn her trust and will ensure that you gain respect and honesty right back from her.

8. Dependable

If you say you will do something, do it. If she needs you to do something for her, do your best, even if you have no idea what you are doing. If she can depend on you to be there to support her when she needs you, she will feel a lot more secure and loved in your relationship than if she cannot depend on your for anything. This is especially important when you are going to have a baby as being dependable is how to be a good husband during pregnancy. She will need you the most when she is carrying your baby.

9. Indulgent

Women and children have one thing in common; they love a good pampering. And a good husband knows how to pamper her. Indulging your wife in the things she loves will make her see just how much you care about her. It will win you some points with her, and she is sure to indulge you in the things that you love as well.

10. Humorous

Women are more drawn to men who can make them laugh. A good man knows how to keep his wife and what to say to cheer his wife when she is feeling low. If you also want to keep your wife happy at all times, bring some humour in your life. Make your wife laugh now and then, she will love you dearly.

11. Chivalrous

Some women like to act too independent and tough for the likes of men, but most women would give anything to be with a gentleman. Carry the bags for her, open doors for her and pull out her chair at the restaurant on date night. It makes a difference to a woman when she is treated like a lady.

12. Respectful

A good husband respects his wife and her opinions and beliefs. Understanding, accepting and respecting the fact that your wife is still a separate being than you, who had different ideas, dreams, and opinions, is important in a marriage. You must respect your wife's wishes and her needs. Don't force her to give up on her own dreams to follow yours, but talk things out and see what works for both of you.

13. Selfless

A man who loves his wife is also selfless. Loving another person is the most selfless thing anyone can do. When you really love someone, you put them first. This is a big difference between love and infatuation. A husband who loves his wife will be able to celebrate her successes.

Some men find the success of their wives to be a very bitter pill to swallow as they always expect that their own success should come first. Don't be that guy.

14. Active

A good husband is active and he helps his wife at home too. It becomes hard for a woman of today to balance work and home. But a good husband helps his wife in housework. As her husband, it would help her out so much if you were more active in the home, cleaning up after yourself and helping out with some of the chores. So, if you love your wife, help her too.

15. Decisive

A good man is decisive. He knows what he has to do. A good man considers his wife's opinions and values his own opinions and takes the right decision for the family. Do not be the type of man who cannot make a decision as that is not a good quality to have.

16. Believes in Who He Is

A good man and good husband never shies away in being himself. If you love your wife, be who you really are. It may seem like there are so many things that you need to work on, but for the most part, be yourself. You don't need to fake anything or make up stories to impress her. She loves you for who you are, and there is no need to pretend to be like anybody else.

17. Good Team Player

A good husband is also a team player. As a husband, you must realise that you and your wife are a team. Being a good team player is vital in a marriage. It is not always about you, but you need to think about another person as well. When you have children, this becomes all the more important. Never undermine her decisions in front of your children, but talk to her in private if you don't agree with something she did. Showing your children that the two of you are a team will prevent them from trying to take advantage of the situation and will teach them what a real relationship is like between man and woman.

18. Mindful

A good husband is mindful. He remembers the important days of his life. Men usually forget important dates, so if you are that type of man, do something to help you remember all the important dates. Set reminders for the important birthdays, anniversaries and other big events that you need to be aware of. Your wife may not have the time to remind you of everything.

19. Kind

Kindness in a man is a very appealing quality to women. She will know that you will never hurt her and that you will always do what is best for her and your family. Kindness towards others will certainly make your wife so proud of you that you may find her bragging about it to all her friends.

20. Never Judges

A good man never judges his wife for her flaws. The golden rule in all marriages is that you need to walk a mile in someone else's shoes to know what they are going through before you judge them. Your wife may have done something that you don't agree with, but if you stop and show understanding by applying the golden rule, you will be able to talk it out with her and come to an agreeable solution.

You should always treat your spouse the way that you want to be treated, i.e., with love and respect. A happy marriage takes quite a bit of work from both the partners. We hope that the above tips will help you play your part to make your marriage a happy one.

Chapter 10

WAYS TO BE A MUCH BETTER FATHER

The 18-year task of raising a child from birth to adulthood is one of man's most noble journeys—and greatest challenges. One moment, you're figuring out how to build a crib and plastic toys, and in a blink, you're waxing on about the dangers of Fireball shots.

What makes fatherhood most complicated is not just the constant barrage of decisions, pressures, and circumstances that demand your attention. ("No, Ms. Principal, I'm not aware that Bart sketches Greek statues of naked men and women in his textbook during class.")

It's that every family is an experiment involving so many variables.

Every child is different, and so is every father. You've got sporty dads and artsy dads. Serious dads and goofy dads.

Tough dads and pushover dads. Meaning: What you may think is best for your kid because of who you are may not actually be the case because of who they are.

A good father has to be part coach and cop, preacher and teacher, friend and foe. And he has to walk that tightrope with two goals in mind: One, help create a dynamite kid.

And two, develop a relationship that will last a lot longer than the 6,574 days of their childhood. So the question becomes: How do you navigate all the tricky terrain that comes with parenting, disciplining, teaching, and bonding so that you do what's best for your kids in the long run, while also ensuring that you end up on the good side of their memories, and not the "he was such a prick" one?

It's not about making 180-degree changes in parenting philosophy or in personality traits. It's about doing the little things—the things that teach them, that entertain them, that challenge them, and that show them that you give two hoots.

After all, a child's mind is one big game of connect-the-dots. Every dot you put in their memory is what forms the big picture.

It's the little moments that mean the most. Kids don't need big flashy experiences. They need deep relationships with caring adults.

The best way to do it is with your time. When kids feel as if dad is paying attention, that's when the best fathering happens.

Here, are ways to make a pretty big difference.

Shut. It. Off.

According to the Pew Research Center, 48 percent of fathers say they spend too little time with their kids. That's all the more reason to resist your check-your-phone habit when you are with them. Dads almost never put their phones down. Even brief breaks pay huge dividends.

When you're engaged with your kids, ditch your device—so your children get the message that your eyes and mind are with them and not with what J.J. Watt is tweeting.

Talk a Lot When They're Little

Talk out loud, talk to yourself, talk to them, read them books. Even when they're of the age when they'll have no idea what "hmm, we're out of mustard" means, it's good for their brains for you to say it out loud, rather than just think of it. One study found that a father's vocabulary had a stronger effect on a child's language development than a mother's.

Use the Crib-Cry Rule—Even When They're Teens

Many parents advocate letting babies cry it out in their cribs—to help self-soothe and learn to fall asleep on their own. That same philosophy works with older kids (without the crying and without the cribs). When your child gets upset at you ("Dad, you're the only one who won't let me wear ripped jeans!"), your inclination may to be to engage in a verbal battle of rights and wrongs. The better play? Walking away for a moment.

"If I get frustrated, I just leave the room for a few minutes. It lets me re-group and then jump back in," says Jason Greene, founder of One Good Dad. "Men in particular want to be defensive, step up to the plate and start swinging. But if you step out of the batter's box and calm down, you can better try to fix things." Besides quelling the specific situation, it pays other dividends as well.

Create "Your" Game

One day, Greene took his son to play work on soccer drills in an urban handball court. They passed the ball around, but it evolved into the two of them playing handball rules with a soccer ball. That game started organically, but is now a tradition that's theirs and only theirs.

Engage, Maverick, Engage!

From day one, embrace everything that comes with fatherhood—diapers, debates, decisions, diarrhea duty, all of it. A British study found that when men were confident about their role in parenthood—especially their role as father in the early years—that led to fewer behavioral problems as adolescents.

Don't Whine About Work

While it's good to share work conflicts with your partner, think about what happens if every family dinner consists of you complaining about knucklehead executives. You're showing your kids that work is something to be despised.

But if you can speak of what you love about you do, you're teaching them to do what you ultimately want them to do—to pursue a career that they're passionate about.

There's a Time for "No Rules"

Unlike most aspects of our lives where we expect a winner and loser (sports, politics), playing with your young kids doesn't always have to have an outcome. So no, you don't always need to keep score. That means more playgrounds, more hikes, and more make-it-up-as-we-go-along games. One study shows that fathers who play with their kids in this way have to deal with fewer behavior problems down the line.

Do More Chores

Being diligent about cleaning the peanut butter off the spoon before putting it in the dishwasher isn't just about having an equitable distribution of household chores. The fact that you do laundry, clean toilets, make dinner, and know exactly where the eff the Lysol is stored communicates something bigger. A Canadian study found that daughters grow up with greater career aspirations when the fathers share more of the work around the house.

Tradition Trumps Grandiose

Kids will remember a lot about growing up. Favorite teachers, first pets, the time you embarrassed them by wearing Crocs to a parent-teacher conference. But they'll also remember the actions that became traditions. One friend of mine takes his son to the Waffle House before school on the first Friday of the month. Another friend chooses one day a year—randomly—when he takes a wrong turn on the way to school and plays hooky at the amusement park.

Follow These Rules

Expose them to a variety of foods early—unless one of those foods is a grape Fanta. Slip them a $5 somtimes just because—unless you suspect it will become beer money. Embrace the power of puppies—unless you already have three of them. Always have a spare phone charger on hand—unless they've already lost or broken three of them. Dance with them—unless you're a chaperone for their prom.*

* Do not be a chaperone for their prom

Zip It

The most toxic environment in the world, besides #politicaltwitter: The sidelines of a youth sporting event.

That's mainly because there's a subset of parents who think that their mission at that moment is hooting from the stands with advice, instructions, and ump-hating snipes. The best thing you can do—as hard as it is—is to let the coaches coach and the refs ref. And the children play. Kids are now constantly looking to the sidelines for feedback instead of focusing on the coaches and playing.

The result: They feel micromanaged and criticized, she says, when they thought they were supposed to be doing something fun. In effort to make them better in sports, parental yappiness is the exact thing that drives them away.

Put 'Em to Work Early

Want to prepare them for life responsibilities? (Nod your head yes.) Put them in the kitchen. Even 2-year-olds can help stir the scrambled eggs. "It was important for my wife and me for our kids to learn how to cook; we read that Millennials are getting out of the house and not knowing how to cook," says Greene, who has four kids (the oldest of whom is 13 and just made spaghetti dinner for the family).

Harness the Power of Their Phones

Kids and their phones. They have so much access—to everything. Instead of being paranoid about them being exposed to the horrors of the world, do what one of my friends does: Use sensitive moments that they'll see on social media as talking points about race, violence, harassment, politics, whatever it is. After all, if you've made the decision that they're old enough for a smartphone, you've made the decision that they're old enough to see anything that may pop up on it.

Ask More, Decide Less

Dad is the default decision-maker when it comes to play time. But instead of saying, "wanna play H-O-R-S-E?" try this: "What do you want to do?"

Dads often dictate the terms of play. Time together is even more meaningful when dads play what the child wants to.

Adapt Your Discipline

There's some thinking that your discipline style has to be consistent all the time. But some research indicates that you ought to be more pliable—adjusting how you react to the behavior, not the mandated household rules. An Oklahoma State University study showed that sometimes kids need punishment while other times negotiation leads to a better outcome. (Of course, the key is to be on the same page with the other adult in your household before you dole out the disciplinary decisions.)

Rock On with the Silly Faces

When fathers are the jokers, they often get dismissed as not taking family life seriously, or that they're avoiding the real issues, or that they're just trying to make peace rather than resolve issues. But studies show that dads who can make young children laugh, even during stressful times, actually benefit their emotional development.

Take Them to a Place Where Nobody Speaks Your Language

Greene says he loves taking the family to non-English-speaking countries, because it helps them develop other skills in independence, as they have to try to order food or navigate transportation systems (provided the parents involve them in the action, which he and his wife do). One of his favorite stories: On a bus in Barcelona, everyone got on, but the family got separated because it was so crowded.

From afar, Greene saw his son, 11 at the time, get out of his seat and offer a seat to an elderly woman. She spoke broken English, and he spoke broken Spanish, so it took some time for the woman to figure out what he was doing. When she did realize, the two started conversing the best they could. "It was a really nice moment between two people with nothing in common," Greene says. The lesson for the kids: "You can handle pretty much anything after you've been to a strange place," he says. "Things don't seem that big when you come back home."

"Next To" equals "Talk With"

Greene spends quality time with his kids in side-by-side activities: Playing video games with his son and getting a mani-pedi with his daughter. Both situations, he says, gives them a relaxed and easy way to talk. "Those will be nice memories for the two of us spending time together having out nails done, sitting and talking for 30 minutes about whatever is on her mind."

Use Various Teaching Tools

Many fathers want to pass along their wisdom by giving straight advice: Do this because this is what works. That's all well and good, but you can be more effective but altering your styles the professional advice-givers do.

Preachers tell stories and let the audience reflect on the meaning. Teachers ask questions to allow the students come up with the answer themselves. Not every piece of advice has to come loudly and directly from the all-caps FATHER.

Think for a Second About the End Game

Not every decision you make will be welcome. You won't always be liked. And sometimes, you'll have more conflict than Roger Goodell's inbox. But in the end, no matter what you go through, you do want your kids to turn out well—and know that you cared. So maybe, when things get tough, it would help to think back on a popular fatherhood quote that appears in the book, The Book Thief by Markus Zusak: "Sometimes I think my papa is an accordion. When he looks at me and smiles and breathes, I hear the notes." Which, in the end, is probably how we'd like all of our kids to feel.

www.ingramcontent.com/pod-product-compliance
Ingram Content Group UK Ltd.
Pitfield, Milton Keynes, MK11 3LW, UK
UKHW041850190726
13854UKWH00002B/815

9 798454 133092